THE DEVELOPMENT OF PHILOSOPHY IN JAPAN

A DISSERTATION PRESENTED TO
THE FACULTY OF PRINCETON UNIVERSITY
IN CANDIDACY FOR THE DEGREE
OF DOCTOR OF PHILOSOPHY

BY
TSUNEZO KISHINAMI

Published by Left of Brain Books

Copyright © 2021 Left of Brain Books

ISBN 978-1-396-32088-0

First Edition

All rights reserved. No part of this publication may be reproduced, distributed, or transmitted in any form or by any means, including photocopying, recording, or other electronic or mechanical methods, without the prior written permission of the publisher, except in the case of brief quotations embodied in critical reviews and certain other noncommercial uses permitted by copyright law. Left of Brain Books is a division of Left of Brain Onboarding Pty Ltd.

Table of Contents

I. INTRODUCTION	1
II. THE MENTAL CHARACTERISTICS OF THE JAPANESE	2
III. THE STAGES OF PHILOSOPHICAL DEVELOPMENT	5
1. The First Stage	5
2. The Second Stage	9
3. The Third Stage	13
IV. THE RELATION OF RELIGION TO THE PHILOSOPHICAL DEVELOPMENT IN JAPAN	15
V. SOCIAL AND ETHICAL PROBLEMS IN RELATION TO THE PHILOSOPHICAL DEVELOPMENT	19
VI. THE PHILOSOPHICAL DEVELOPMENT VIEWED FROM THE SIDE OF EDUCATION—SOCIETIES AND PERIODICALS	21
VII. CONCLUDING REMARKS	23
BIBLIOGRAPHY	26

I. INTRODUCTION

The real beginning of the philosophical development in Japan is the time of the so-called Revolution of Meiji,[1] though the Oriental philosophy of life was well developed many centuries earlier and prepared the Japanese mind in complex, manifold and subtle ways for the new study of the Occidental philosophy. It is, therefore, barely a half century's progress that mainly concerns our present study. Of course it is too short for the mental development of the race, for a decade of years is only one year to the race development. In fact, the Japanese mind is still in the stage of assimilation. It cannot yet show anything which is worthy to be called a native production in the field of philosophy. It is not, however, without interest to study the mental processes of a people, who, until the middle of the nineteenth century, were entirely secluded from the outer world. A too hasty reception of such dignified thought as the Western philosophy would, indeed, have been open to suspicion. Is there not after all a danger like indigestion or suffocation of the mind? How and in what manner have the Japanese assimilated the new and difficult thought? What is their merit and what is their defect in philosophical development? What will be their future? These and kindred questions require our careful and faithful investigation. Some may deplore as unduly indulgent the assumption that the Japanese labors in the field of philosophy are deserving of such study. I should claim that their very immaturity may lend added interest to the enquiry and may even serve as a claim to our special attention. But even though my task may be regarded by some as of little consequence, I shall strive to describe it in a faithful manner. As Augustine has said, "Little things are little things; but faithfulness in little things is something great."

---

[1] 1868 A.D.

II. THE MENTAL CHARACTERISTICS OF THE JAPANESE

It is helpful, nay, even necessary for our present task to have a general knowledge of the mental characteristics of the Japanese. The mental play in the theatre of a nation can be fully understood only in and through our thorough familiarity with some main and significant traits of its actors. If we neglect this preliminary study we can hardly penetrate into the real nature of what has been happening.

It seems to me that Mr. Dening is quite adequate when he describes the Japanese characteristics in the following manner:

"Neither their past history nor their prevailing taste show any tendency to idealism. They are lovers of the practical and real; neither the fancies of Goethe nor the reveries of Hegel are to their liking. Our poetry and our philosophy and the mind that appreciates them are alike the results of a net-work of subtle influences to which the Japanese are comparative strangers. It is maintained by some, and we think justly, that the lack of idealism in the Japanese mind renders the life of even the most cultivated a mechanical, humdrum affair when compared with that of Westerners. The Japanese can not understand why our controversialists should wax so fervent over psychological, ethical, religious, and philosophical questions, failing to perceive that this fervency is the result of the intense interest taken in such subjects. The charms that the cultivated Western mind finds in the world of fancy and romance, in questions themselves, irrespective of their practical bearings, are for the most part unintelligible to the Japanese."

There are abundant proofs of this practical tendency of Japanese thought. One of the most obvious instances is the fact that when the Japanese came in contact with Western culture, they first of all learned those arts and science, especially the medical and the military, which are most directly connected with individual and national existence. In so doing they revealed a quite remarkable power of using their new knowledge to good practical purpose. Indeed the Japanese tend toward utilitarianism in the wider sense of that term. As Mr. Dening has said, they are lovers of the practical and the real. They tend to consider that what is real is true and that what is true is real. We find them saying that "proof is better than argument." This tendency has had such free play that the people have in many respects shown themselves prone to a materialism or naturalism which conflicts with the Christian view of life and which places added difficulties in the way of their evangelization.

The development of philosophical ideas in Japan also illustrates this practical tendency. A philosophy of conduct, which has derived its inspiration chiefly from the Confucian teaching, ruled the people for many centuries. As Dr. Dyer states in his work "Dai Nippon,"[2] the chief end of education in Japan was to build up character. This practical, or virtue-centric tendency has been insisted upon by one of the most typical philosophers of Old Japan:[3]

"Scholar is a name for virtue, not for arts. Literature is an art, and a man with an inborn genius for it has no difficulty in becoming a man of letters. But though proficient in letters, he is not a scholar if he be lacking in virtue. He is only an ordinary person knowing letters. An illiterate man with virtue is not an ordinary person. He is a scholar without letters."

Not only Nakae but almost all scholars emphasised "to be" in order "to do." In other words, they all strove to realize the true self and regarded it as the ultimate end of life.

The same trait is obvious in the development of Buddhism in Japan. Owing to its extramundane nature and its pessimistic tone Buddhism did not at first appeal to the native mind, except that its rites and arts found a response in their superstitions and aesthetic nature. But when the people came to reflect on life, and were dissatisfied with its present state, especially at a period when men's chief business was to fight and women's to weep, Buddhism, with its doctrine of Karma and Nirvana, gave solution to their problems and salvation to their restless souls. Calmness, patience and benevolence are its meritorious outcome; and are written large in Japanese life.

It is worth while to notice the rise of a new sect called "Shinshiu" in 1266. The Shinshin has been called the "Protestantism of Japan." Its teaching is akin to Christianity. It puts stress on salvation by faith. It teaches that Amida, god of gods, is a merciful being, and that his mercy is so abundant that any person, however sinful and wicked, if only he pray with true and earnest heart for his salvation, can be saved by merciful Amida. This sect, unlike other sects, is in direct contact with actual life. Its priests may marry, and they are free to eat

---

[2] Pg. 44
[3] Toju Nakae. See Mr. Uchimura's "Representative Men of Japan." (Pp. 139-178.)

both flesh and fish. It is the most powerful of the Japanese sects; its temples are large and magnificent, are found in the most crowded parts of the cities, and are thronged day and night with earnest worshippers. In opposition to this sect is the "Zenshin" or "contemplative" sect. It is akin to Spinoza's ethical teaching, seeking salvation through the acquisition of truth. Not faith but reason, not heart but mind, this sect regards as essential for the living of a good life. This sect, inspires the educated people, while the Shinshin sect meets the need of the common people. Both, however, agree in their practical tendency and close attachment to life.

This tendency is even more obviously revealed in Bushido, a moral principle of the Samurai, and in the popular philosophy of Shingaku. Both are an outcome of genuine Japanese life in so far as that has been moulded by the intermingled influences of Confucianism, Buddhism and Shintoism. But that is a matter which I cannot here discuss in detail. In Dr. Nitobe's famous work "Bushido" and Dr. Knox's "Japanese Life in Town and Country," there is ample evidence, sufficient to convince every fair-minded reader, that these movements are both practical in type and genuinely Japanese in character.

The Japanese, in short, are a predominantly practical people. Being practical, as Dr. Takayama has well said, their single aim is life. This is at once their defect and their merit; defect, because it may hinder the development of their speculative thinking; and merit, because it keeps intact the vital relation between life and thought. It is a question, however, how far this practical tendency has proved a hindrance. Indeed it may be argued that it has actually aided in the development of Japanese philosophy. Japan, so long secluded from the world, and suddenly awakened as from a dream, had good reason to hold fast to its anchorage in the practical necessities of life. But before we enter upon a discussion of this subject, let us see how the Japanese with their remarkably practical tendency did in fact accomplish their philosophical development. The above question will then be more easily solved; nay, we shall find it already answered.

III. THE STAGES OF PHILOSOPHICAL DEVELOPMENT

We must constantly bear in mind the preliminary or embryonic stage in the philosophical development of Japan, that is, the development of Oriental thought in Old Japan, prior to the Revolution of Meiji.[4] If we consider the great period of time over which this preliminary development extends and the degree to which it has moulded the Japanese mind, we shall not be in danger of underestimating the part which it is destined to play in all modern Japanese movements. But with this word of caution, I must leave it undiscussed. It falls outside the scope of our present enquiry.

There are three main stages in the philosophical development of New Japan. The first stage, during which French and English thought was influential, covers the period from the beginning of Meiji to the latter part of the second decade. The second stage, during which German thought was influential, begins amidst the prevailing influence of previous thought and extends to the end of the fourth decade. The third stage, during which the subject of study was widened and interest among the people was expanded, appears at the end of the fourth decade and continues to the present day. These three stages have as their respective backgrounds the corresponding tendencies of thought on politics, social problems, education and religion. These backgrounds make the development of philosophy peculiar and complex in each of its stages.

I. The First Stage

(Approximately 1868-1886)

The first stage of philosophical development in Japan is, broadly speaking, a period of Enlightenment. For the Japanese at this time, having been awakened by the new light of the culture and science of the West, lost their confidence in the traditional authorities and powers. They began to recognize the right of individual reasoning in the various spheres, political, social, moral

---

[4] 1868 A.D.

and religious. They dethroned custom and enthroned truth. "Truth and nothing but truth" was the watchword of this time. Anything and everything, therefore, that was new and rational seemed acceptable to them, and at once struck root into the soil of the Japanese mind. This *Zeitgeist* is fully embodied in Emperor Mutsuhito himself. On ascending the throne in 1868, the young emperor enunciated the fundamental principles of his government in the form of a solemn oath, which has since then been known as "the Five Articles of the Imperial Oath." The articles are as follows:

(1) Deliberative assemblies should be established, and all members of government should be controlled by public opinion.

(2) All classes, high or low, should unite in vigorously carrying out the programme upon what the government may decide.

(3) Officials, civil and military, and all common people should, as far as may be possible, be allowed to fulfil their just desires, so that they may not be divided by discontent.

(4) Uncivilized customs of former times should be broken through, and everything should be based upon the just and equitable principles of nature.

(5) Knowledge should be sought for throughout the world, that the welfare of the empire may be promoted.

These articles, like the Declaration of Independence, reveal the spirit of a revolutionary age. This is especially true of the last two articles, which re-echo the rationalistic unhistorical character of the eighteenth century European Enlightenment.

The introduction of Western philosophy into Japan occurred under the influence and inspiration of this general movement, but took place in a very gradual manner. Mr. Miyake has suggested that philosophical studies might have developed more rapidly had the United States been less essentially practical, and the existing American philosophies been less closely allied with religion. This view, though it may be true in certain respects, seems to me to be at least one-sided. As I have already argued, I think it was both natural and necessary that the Japanese, temperamentally a practical people, should first turn their attention to the medical and military arts and sciences, and should not until later occupy themselves with pure speculative learning. The development, has indeed, depended upon external circumstances, but in much greater degree upon native needs. It is a noteworthy fact and can not be accounted mere chance that Prof. Wayland's "Ethics" and "Political Economy" were widely read by the Japanese before and after the Revolution of Meiji. This already reveals the practical and virtue-centric tendency of their natural interests.

It was in the sixth year of Meiji, *i.e.*, 1873, that a philosophical course, was for the first time, opened in the Kaisei-Gakko, the former institution of the Tokyo Imperial University. Prof. J. Summers gave his lectures on logic, using Fowler's "Deductive Logic" and Mill's "System of Logic" as textbooks. The next year Professor Syle was added to the staff. He taught psychology, using as textbooks Hopkin's "Study of Man" and Haven's "Mental Philosophy."

Two years later Dr. M. Toyama, who had studied at Michigan University, was appointed the first Japanese professor in Philosophy. He introduced Spencer's thought in its various lines. The next year, *i.e.*, 1877, Prof. E. S. Morse introduced the evolution theory of Darwin and Huxley in a manner which gave it influence and currency. Prof. Fenollosa, who in 1878 came from Harvard University, gave lectures on religion based on Spencer's Sociology. Mr. Fukuzawa's "Jiji-shogen, or Random Thoughts of the Time," which is largely based on Galton's theory of heredity, reflects the prevalent tendencies of this epoch. Though Christianity had already begun to strike root in the native mind, and though heated discussions had appeared between Christians and those who followed Darwin and Spencer, the general mind rather tended to favor the latter, proving the justice of Professor Chamberlain's words: "They now bow down before the shrine of Herbert Spencer."

There is another factor noticeable in the philosophical development at this period, namely, the influence of Utilitarianism. The group of the Keio-Gijuku,[5] now Keio University, gave chief attention and favor to the teaching of Bentham and Mill.

The most widely spread and most influential type of thought was, no doubt, that of the French Enlightenment. It prevailed not with this or that group of thinkers, but among the nation at large. The nation had become acquainted with the Western nations and with their various forms of government. The demand for liberty, equality and the individual's right to judge things by his own reason then naturally arose; and driven by an inward

---

[5] Founded by Mr. Fukuzawa a few years before the Revolution of Meiji.

need for these things people found the great teachers in that line,—such teachers as Voltaire, Montesquieu, and Rousseau. The introduction of this French thought was made by those natives who studied in France. Of these Mr. T. Nakae was the most noted. He translated Rousseau's "Social Contract" in 1882.[6] The French thought was so influential at this time that it inspired the Liberal party and through this party the whole nation, and hastened the establishment of constitutional government in Japan.

The Japanese Enlightenment differs from the Greek Enlightenment and resembles that of the eighteenth century in its predominantly practical character. The Greek Sophists were skeptical. They despaired of solving the problem of the universe, and finding no satisfactory objective criterion to distinguish between right and wrong, appealed either to the authority of the customary or to the varying judgments of individual men. The Japanese, on the other hand, held firmly to the conviction that there is universal truth, and that it is attainable by man's reason. This is shown in the Emperor Mutsuhito's announcement that "Knowledge should be sought for throughout the world." That declaration rests on the conviction that truth is universal, and that we possess the power of discovering it. Unfortunately or fortunately, however, the movement lasted only little more than one decade of years, and before it could develop its full content the reactionary movement had begun to make its appearance, and the philosophical development entered upon the second stage.

Here a question naturally arises: "Why was the Enlightenment in Japan so short?" Several points may be noted. First, the common people, or mass of men, were perfectly satisfied with the verdict of common sense under whose guidance they made no extreme adventure in thought and action, and consequently no grievous mistakes. With regard to the basis of ethics, likewise, it may be safely affirmed that ethical opinions were, in general, very moderate. Owing to their practical tendency they always took account of their effect upon life. They were constructive and avoided any extreme thought which is destructive and might endanger actual life.

Secondly, the reactionary spirit arose and was the chief factor in bringing the movement to its end. In fact, the introduction of Western culture and

---

[6] He also translated some other French books; e.g., Fouillées "Histoire de la Philosophie."

science into Japan moved hand in hand with the development of political affairs. The restoration of Imperial power over the whole nation by compelling the people to make some sort of revolution in the various spheres, political, moral, social and religious, etc., supplied an opportunity for the manifestation of individualism of the modern Enlightenment type. But when these changes had been made and the new modes of government were firmly established, the people naturally began to reflect, and came to be aware of their native conditions as these had historically developed. In other words, the Japanese national consciousness was awakened. This turn of current thought, strange to say, was hastened by the Enlightenment movement itself. For in contributing to the establishment of constitutional government, it aided in supplying the conditions under which a greater degree of self-consciousness could be attained. When Japan became truly aware of itself, its gaze inevitably returned upon its past and the Enlightenment, in its cosmopolitan character, was at an end.

2. The Second Stage

(Approximately 1886-1905)

In the second stage in the development of philosophy in Japan German thought is dominant. While the constitution was being drawn up various institutions of European origin were studied, and the opinions of experts were asked for. Among those to whom we largely owe the adjustment of State affairs was Dr. Stein of Austria, who taught our senior statesmen the idea of a State and how to manage it. At the same time public opinion began to favor German principles in politics, mainly because the institutions of Germany were akin to those of Japan. The military system also was fashioned on the German model, though previously it had been fashioned on the French model. Moreover, from the middle of the second decade of Meiji, the students sent abroad by the government prosecuted their studies mostly in Germany, and on their return were looked upon as leaders of contemporary Japan. In these various ways German thought came to permeate the fields of politics, education, law, music and the various sciences. This atmosphere of philo-

Germanism took its course in Japan side by side with the national consciousness which encouraged the renaissance of national classics.

It was as early as 1880 that Professor Cooper first introduced Kant's critical philosophy to Japan. Professor Fenollosa also taught at this time Hegel's logic. In 1885 and 1886 Professor Knox,[7] professor at Meiji-Gakuin, gave his lectures in the Tokyo Imperial University. Professor Busse, who is now professor at Königsberg University, Germany, followed Professor Knox. Both of them tended toward Lotze's thought. In 1890 Dr. T. Inone[8] returned from Germany after some years' study at Leipzig. He was chiefly influenced by the teaching of Wundt. Two years previously, Dr. Motosa, on returning from America after some years' study at Boston University and Johns Hopkins, had introduced psychophysics. This study also drew the natives toward Wundt, and his influence became very considerable. Four years later, *i.e.*, in 1894, Professor Koeber took the chair of Professor Busse after his resignation and holds it at the present time. He gave his courses, at this time, on Schopenhauer and Hartmann. Thus in this period German thought in one or another of its diverse forms prevailed in philosophical circles.

While German thought was influencing the Japanese, the general tendency, as might be expected, gradually changed from that of the Enlightenment spirit to that of the Romantic movement. As the Enlightenment spirit declined the conservative and retrospective spirit began to take its place among the people who were so youthful in the previous stage. In some sense, indeed, this is the period of the awakening of the self-consciousness that accompanies adolescence—complex and full of danger. The Japanese mind, as we have noted, had been influenced over a very long period by Buddhism, and that left as a permanent deposit a deep pathos and seriousness of spirit. A brighter more confident attitude had temporarily appeared in the decade of the Enlightenment, but now that the current was altered, Buddhism revived. The classical literature was recalled with enthusiasm. The general interest in literary matters greatly increased; and in dissatisfaction with mere translations from foreign tongues the desire arose for

---

[7] Cf., Professor Knox's "A Japanese Philosopher."

[8] Dr. T. Inone lectured in Paris in 1897, upon the development of philosophical thought in Japan. Since that time he has been devoting himself to the completion of his study of Japanese philosophy.

original and native works. This period has therefore been entitled the "Renaissance of Meiji." It not only represents the revival of the Japanese classics; but also represents, like Romanticism in modern Europe, what may be called the "Renaissance of Wonder." As a reaction against the rationalism of the previous period it bears the sign of anti-intellectualism, which led, however, in the next stage, to a higher and deeper view of the true nature and function of thought or reason.

This quasi-Romanticism helped philosophical development by the close contact it established between literature and philosophy. Philosophers like Schopenhauer, Hartmann and Nietzsche came to exercise great influence in general thought. At this time also many young natives became interested in the study of aesthetics. Especial mention may be made of the writings on this subject of Dr. Takayama, Dr. Mori and Dr. Tsubouchi. The rise of literature, in short, was largely inspired by philosophical thought, and the advancement of literature, in turn, gave a stimulus to the development of philosophy.

There are two other factors that call for notice in this stage of philosophical development; namely, historicism and nationalism. Both appear in the reaction against the Enlightenment movement. Nationalism is opposed to individualism and historicism to the revolutionary spirit. In their development they took on various different aspects, but nationalism developed chiefly on the line of ethical or educational interest; while historicism contributed to the adoption of an historical method in literature and in scientific studies.

Between 1890 and 1895 several histories of Japanese literature were published. The historical study of Buddhism was, for the first time, attempted by the party called "New Buddhists." The historical study of the Japanese arts was also attempted.[9] These are indications that the Japanese had come to be aware of the important truth of historical continuity.

As to nationalism, we may recognize that its inspiration came direct from German thought. But it is none the less true, that the native mind welcomed the nationalist point of view owing to its affinity with the political and social needs of Japan at this time. Nationalism first appeared as the "Conservative Party," whose chief representatives were Mr. Shiga and Dr. Miyake. They

---

[9] E.g., Dr. Takayama wrote his "History of Japanese Arts."

published in 1887 a new magazine called "Nihonjin" in which they warned the Japanese not to imitate other nations, blindly forgetting their own meritorious qualities as recorded in history. A group who adopted a policy called "Japanism" arose some ten years later. Their message according to its foremost propounder, Dr. Takayama, is not "conservation" but "criticism," that is to say, to criticise everything according to the standard of the national needs, regardless whether what is criticized be old or new, native or foreign. The attitude of Japanism is, he maintains, distinctively critical in contrast with the uncritical conservatism of the old party. This nationalism alike in its more conservative and its more liberal form, found opportunity to enrich its content and to define its position both in the solving of internal problems and in the constantly recurring conflicts with other nations. It has been greatly intensified by the wars with China and Russia.

This national spirit came to be so strong that a hot controversy arose in 1892 between the conservative thinkers and those converted to Christianity. The points in the indictment of Christianity were formulated as follows:

(1) Christianity pretends to be a universal religion, and does not recognize national difference. This contradicts the fundamental teaching of the edict which is strongly national and patriotic.

(2) Christian morality is founded upon a supernatural belief in Divinity. This is contrary to the practical and nationalistic basis of our morality.

(3) The love of Christianity is universal and does not admit special duties toward ruler and parents. This is diametrically opposed to the cardinal virtues, filial piety and loyalty, as insisted upon in the edict.

This representation of Christianity may perhaps be regarded as too clearly erroneous and partial. The conservative thinkers, however, in their enthusiastic adoption of the nationalist standpoint, seemed to themselves to be inevitably led to this interpretation of Christianity.

To conclude: in this prolonged second stage, the people of Japan passed from the Enlightenment to the Romanticist attitude. Their Romanticist attitude found expression for itself on the one hand in historicism, and on the other in nationalism.

3. The Third Stage

(Approximately, 1905 to the present time.)

Dr. Kuwaki calls this period that of Subjectivism, adopting the term used by Prof. K. Lamprecht. As he has explained, the spirit of this period, like that of Europe in the beginning of the nineteenth century, is marked by self-consciousness. We find here, as in the history of Greek thought, a change of current, ebb and flow. We have seen that the two main achievements of the preceding stage, were historicism and nationalism. Toward the end of that stage, however, the Japanese have come round to the opposite of the first stage. Rationalism has now gone and reliance upon the instinctive has taken its place. The atmosphere which was so fresh during the first stage, the Enlightenment period, has become heavy and oppressive; and many are led to seek their salvation in religion, especially in Christianity. This new spiritual demand may be characterized by such words as "restlessness" or "self-knowledge." They are very prevalent in the literature of the time. With this changing attitude the second stage is ended and our present stage is before us with its new message and new hope.

In proportion to the general progress in experience and in knowledge, the philosophical interest came to be deepened as well as expanded. The native thinkers began at this time to present their careful expositions to the public. For instance Dr. Hatano published his "Study on Spinoza" in 1910. Last year Mr. Watsuji completed his study of Nietzsche, and Mr. Inage his exposition of Eucken's thought. Professor Kuwaki also published several works among which his "Gendai Schicho Jikko" is the most notable. It is marked by clearness and scholarly treatment of modern thought under the heads of Realism, Agnosticism, Naturalism, Historicism, Impressionism, Pragmatism and New Realism.

There are many translations of philosophical works. Plato's works were translated by Mr. T. Kimura in 1903. Eucken's works and Bergson's works have been translated by young students. Dr. Anezaki, now lecturer at Harvard University, has recently translated Schopenhauer's "Welt als Wille und Vorstellung." Many other works were also translated, *e.g.,* works by Bowne, Fullerton, Hibben, Höffding, James, and Wundt. We must, however, remember that there are many important works which are read by the Japanese with great interest, and which yet for one or another reason are not translated into Japanese. We must bear in mind also that most of the Japanese students who interest themselves in philosophical study are able to use for their purpose at least either English, German or French; and this perhaps partly accounts for the fact that the translation of foreign works into Japanese is decreasing in number though certainly it is advancing in quality; while, on the other hand, the native works are increasing year after year.[10] Thus far we have studied the stages of philosophical development in Japan viewed from the point of historical continuity. There are, however, still other problems which have not been dealt with, and some points which, though already briefly touched upon, need more detailed treatment. To these I may now proceed.

---

[10] The following statistical table confirms these remarks:

(years)	(translation)	(native works)
1877	232	4.745
1882	241	8.751
1887	692	8.885
1892[1]	173	21.409
1897	141	25.381
1898	9	21.097
1899	180	21.455
1900	111	18.505
1901	35	19.431
1902	8	23.349
1903	17	24.738
1904	28	26.582

[1] Japan entered the International Union of Copyright Reservation in 1888.

IV. THE RELATION OF RELIGION TO THE PHILOSOPHICAL DEVELOPMENT IN JAPAN

There are three religions in Japan; Shintoism, Buddhism and Christianity. Shintoism did not play a very important part in the development of philosophy, except in connection with ethical problems. Even in that field, Confucianism played the more important part. Shintoism, however, cooperated with Confucianism in forming the national spirit. For a long time it drew numerous pilgrims to the high mountains or to retired valleys. Their superstition was thus mingled with the sacred touch of nature as well as with some sort of hero worship. This habit of pilgrimage, though having no very direct or immediate effect upon life, certainly influenced the national morality and especially the spirit of "Bushido." The tenets of Shintoism, as Dr. Nitobe says in his famous "Bushido," cover the two predominating features of the emotional life of our race—Patriotism and Loyalty. As Prof. J. Royce has said in his "Problem of Christianity":

"The Japanese are fond of telling us that their imperial family, and their national life, are coeval with heaven and earth. The boast is cheerfully extravagant; but its relation to a highly developed form of the consciousness of a community is obvious. Here, then, is a consideration belonging to social psychology, but highly important for our understanding of the sense in which a community is or can be possessed of one mental life."

Buddhism is more closely connected with the development of philosophy in Japan. It prepared the people for their new study of Western thought. Also, many Buddhists, while still remaining devout students of their own Oriental literature, themselves prosecuted the study of Occidental philosophy.

During the Enlightenment period Buddhist priests had been severely attacked for their conventionality and for their lack of influence. They were, however, awakened partly by this attack and partly by the appearance of Christianity as a new rival religion which was now powerfully influencing the Japanese. Compelled to arm themselves with the weapon of knowledge and to take the offensive against the new rival, the Japanese Buddhists were constrained to study the new thought of the West. Their choice of means to meet the situation has been well judged, and has enabled them to take full advantage of the favouring reaction against the unhistorical Enlightenment movement. Availing themselves of every opportunity, the Japanese Buddhists became more and more active in their study and in their social work. In 1876 Dr. Manjo, a priest of the "Shinshiu" sect, together with a friend studied in England under Max Muller. Dr. Manjo returned from England in 1884. In the same year Mr. Kitabatake returned from Germany. When Mr. Hara in 1878 became lecturer at the Tokyo Imperial University he opened the way for the students of the University to devote themselves to Buddhistic study.

The Japanese Buddhists found their most congenial inspiration in Schopenhauer, in Spinoza, and in Hegel's quasi-Pantheism. But their study has not, of course, been confined to these. Dr. E. Inone's "Bukko Katsuron," one of the most influential of the new Buddhist writings, was mainly based on Spencer's Agnosticism. Dr. E. Inone established a philosophical institution in Tokyo for the Buddhist students. Besides this institution several Buddhist universities and colleges were established. The two Buddhist thinkers, Dr. Takayama and Dr. Anezaki, while contributing to the historical and philosophical study of Buddhism, also aided in its more popular appeal. Dr. Takayama was specially interested in Saint Nichiren who has been regarded as the "Saint Paul of Japanese Buddhism." Dr. Anezaki wrote an essay: "How Christianity Appeals to a Japanese Buddhist." He attempts in that essay to show that there are in Buddhism points similar to Christianity, though in their historical developments they have taken very different courses. "These two religions (Christianity and Buddhism), viewed in their respective historical sources, show two uncompromising if not contradictory aspects of the religious experience of mankind." He concisely formulates these different aspects, maintaining that Christianity is more practical and religious, while Buddhism is more speculative and less religious. He further argues that there is an essential similarity under these different aspects, since in both cases personal, moral, evidence of religion rests on the person of the founder. He concludes that Christianity is not foreign to Japanese Buddhism, but is in all its essential features akin to it. I may not pause to examine these views. It is enough for us merely to note the attitude of the Japanese Buddhists and to catch a glimpse of their philosophical interests in the sphere of religion.

In fact, the Japanese Buddhists are striving to meet the demand of the age, adopting the same good means and methods which the Christians have been employing. They are very active in their social work. They are also attempting to give a new and more modern interpretation of their central doctrines. Indeed it may be said that the Japanese Buddhists are to a certain extent reforming their doctrines. It is still a question whether this can be successfully achieved without an open breach with the traditions they represent. At any rate, their former attitude towards Christianity which was hostile and extremely antagonistic, has gradually changed to what may fairly be entitled Christianization, not only on the side of practical reforms but even on the side of doctrine and its interpretation. This change of attitude has strengthened, rather than weakened their interest in philosophical problems; and they continue actively to participate in the development of Japanese philosophical thinking. But Christianity is no less closely bound up with the present development of philosophy in Japan. And to understand the part which it plays we must always bear in mind the many and important missionary colleges and seminaries in which the young natives have been initiated into modem culture and science. Even if nothing be said about the main contribution of Christian missionaries in the sphere of religion, their merits as benefactors of Japanese civilization can never be forgotten.

Christianity in Japan has had many difficulties to face; and these difficulties have changed with the changing conditions. The Christians have fought against Spencer's thought. They have fought against the so-called narrow nationalism. They have fought against materialism. Materialism is not perhaps very active in Japan, but at times the Japanese Haeckels have published their manifestos. Dr. K. Kato, the former president of the Tokyo Imperial University, is one of the leading materialist thinkers. Mr. Nakae's "Zoku-Ichinen-Yuhan," a materialist exposition, was written during the author's fatal sickness and published in 1901, and though not a truly scholarly work, has been widely read. The situation in Japan is now more favorable to Christianity than at any previous period, yet the Christian propaganda has of necessity many great difficulties to overcome. Dr. Schneder, the president of North Japan College, recently addressed the conference of the Federated Missions as follows:

"While Christianity is making a little progress, other great forces like that of nationalism, the revival of Shintoism, the renewed activity of Buddhism, agnostic or anti-moral literature and practical materialism, that seem to work in deadly opposition to it, are growing in strength.... Also the more intimate knowledge which the Japanese people are gaining year by year of the moral and social conditions prevailing in the Christian West, and of the thought-currents of the great universities does not constitute to them an unequivocal argument in favor of Christianity."

Such difficult conditions forced the Japanese Christians to fight hard, and gave little chance for the wholesale conversion of large numbers.[11]

It is a noteworthy fact, however, that some of the most noted Japanese scholars belong to the group of Christian thinkers, or were educated at some mission college, such, for instance, as Professor Nakajima, professor of moral philosophy at the Tokyo Imperial University, Dr. Motora who was professor of psychophysics in the same institution, and Dr. Onishi one of the younger generation.[12] It is no exaggeration to say that the greater part of the students of philosophy in Japan at present are either Buddhists or Christians; and that the atmosphere of religious circles is favorable to philosophical enquiry. These twin brothers of the spirit, religion and philosophy, have not on the whole been hostile in Japan. They have cooperated in their common task.

---

[11] The number of the native converts in the various churches, as given in *The Missionary Review of the World* for the year 1913 (vol. xxvi N. S., p. 474) is as follows:

Protestant	83,638
Roman Catholic	66,689
Greek Catholic	32,246

[12] All three men were educated at Doshisha University. Doshisha was established by J. Niejima in 1875.

V. SOCIAL AND ETHICAL PROBLEMS IN RELATION TO THE PHILOSOPHICAL DEVELOPMENT

The most significant change in social conditions in Japan since the Revolution of Meiji is that belief in freedom and equality has taken the place of the traditional feudalism. In ethical fields the same change is obvious. Individualism is no longer condemned as intrinsically evil. In certain quarters there were, of course, men who were opposed to the new tendency, and held the view that the Japanese, while adopting all material civilization from the West, ought to remain faithful to the traditional views of life. The reaction against the Enlightenment tendency and the awakening of the national consciousness encouraged the conservative party, and from time to time heated discussions have arisen between these two opposed schools. In 1888 the famous edict concerning the moral principle of the Japanese was issued. Some conservative scholars hold the view that this edict is exclusively based on nationalism, and that it denounces individualism. Others have rejected this extreme view and have maintained that the edict neither favors nor rejects either of them. Nationalism has, however, come to prevail in the field of public education. Moreover the wars with China and with Russia have strengthened the nationalist forces, and for a time individualism seems to have been losing favour. Nevertheless the change of social life from the old feudalism to the new individualist system has been steadily modifying the Japanese modes of regarding life. The struggle for existence and the open door of the business career have been playing a wonderful part in reforming the social and ethical ideas of the people. Moreover, universal education open on equal terms to both male and female, rich and poor, has given the young a sense of equality and independence with the accompanying consciousness of human dignity. Thus nationalism has gradually come to make room for individualism; each has been modified in terms of the other.

A heated discussion has recently arisen as to the interpretation of State sovereignty. Professor Minobe and Professor Ichimura held the view that both Emperor and subjects belong to the State, which is the seat of sovereignty. Professor Uesugi attacked this position maintaining that the State belongs to the Emperor, and that the Emperor is therefore himself the sole seat of sovereignty. The conservative standpoint seems to be steadily changing. Prof.

T. Inone, for instance, who for a long time was the champion of nationalism has expressed the conviction that even in Japan the State may be the center of sovereignty, both Emperor and subjects belonging to it. For has not Emperor Nintoku himself declared that his subjects do not belong to him, but that he himself exists for his subjects' sake? Such discussions must ultimately issue in genuinely philosophical discussion of the central problems of ethical and political theory.

VI. THE PHILOSOPHICAL DEVELOPMENT VIEWED FROM THE SIDE OF EDUCATION—SOCIETIES AND PERIODICALS

The Imperial Universities and some other private universities offer courses in philosophy, and almost all mission colleges require the study of logic, ethics, and history of philosophy. [13]

---

[13] The following were the courses offered at the Tokyo Imperial University in 1913.

(Subject)	(hours)	(instructor)
1. Chinese Philosophy	(3)	Prof Hoshino.
2. History of Oriental Philosophy	(3)	Prof.T. Inone.
3. The World and Man	(2)	"
4. Outline of Ethics	(3)	Prof. Makajima.
5. Comparative Study of National Ideals	(3)	"
6. Introduction to Philosophy	(2)	Prof. Koeber.

Connected with a brief history of Occidental philosophy from antiquity to the present time.

7. Kant	(2)	"

With special examination of his smaller treatises and Post Kantian Philosophy.

8. History of Christianity	(2)	Prof. Koeber.
9. Schopenhauer—"Welt als Wille und Vorstellung" "Parerga" (reading and interpretation of selected chapters)	(1)	"
10. Lessing as Poet, Critic and Philosopher (reading his "Nathan der Weise.")	(1)	"
11. Reading of Homer's "Odyssey" and Aeschylus' "Prometheus" for advanced students of Greek	(2)	"
12. Reading of Virgil's Bucolics and Ovid's Metamorphoses	(2)	"
13. Outline of Aesthetics	(2)	Prof.Otsuka.
14. History of Modern Culture	(1)	"
15. Sociology	(4)	Prof.Tatebe.
"	(2)	"
Preceptorial- Reading in Comte's works	(1)	"
16. Outline of Chinese Ethics	(6)	Prof.Matsomoto.
18. Experimental Psychology	(2)	"
19. Metaphysics	(2)	Mr. Kinohisa.
20. History of Metaphysics	(1)	"

But generally speaking, the present facilities for philosophical study are extremely inadequate.

There are three noteworthy philosophical societies in Japan. The first philosophical society was established in 1884; the second, entitled an ethical society, was established in 1896. Both societies have been issuing their periodicals since their establishment. A third, which combines the study of philosophy and ethics, was established recently but has not yet issued any periodical. Besides these periodicals which I have just mentioned there is a semi-philosophical magazine called "Rikugo-Zasshi," which was established by a group of Christian thinkers in 1881. It has made noteworthy contributions to Japanese philosophy, particularly during the period when Dr. Onishi was its chief editor.

---

21. Ethics ....(2)...........Prof. Fukatsukuri.
    " ....(4)..........."
22. Logic..(3)...........Mr.Imafuku.
                                            etc.

VII. CONCLUDING REMARKS

Let us now briefly summarize. The Japanese are a practical people, and being practical they always direct their thought to human life. For a long time they regarded the realization of truth in their life as their final end and highest glory. Naturally, therefore, they came to emphasize virtue above all else. This practical and virtue-centric tendency led the Japanese along a narrow but safe path. Under the influence of this tendency they established the new, more modern and more practical, Buddhist sects. Through this tendency there also arose from Shinto, Buddhist and Confucian sources the so-called "Bushido" and "Shingaku."

When the Japanese came in contact with Western civilization, they at once began to adopt what most directly connected with life or at least what in their eyes seemed to do so: *i.e.*, medical science and military art. From these sciences through the difficult medium of totally foreign languages, they progressed slowly, step by step, to other and related sciences. One of the first results was revolution and reform at home. These eventually issued in the new era of Meiji, *i.e.*, the beginning of New Japan.

Western philosophy was not introduced from America and England until the new government, after an intermediate period of turmoil and struggle, had become firmly established, and until a great body of scientific knowledge had been assimilated, and foreign languages, especially English, had gained greater currency. The introduction of philosophy was the final step in the assimilation of Occidental culture; and the Japanese proceeded in their usual manner to utilize the new philosophy for the furtherance of life. Philosophy, was never for the Japanese a mere toy or an idle imitation. It was regarded by them as the only means of attaining such truth as is necessary in order that life may be more fully and truly realized.

The improvement of military art, the advancement of scientific knowledge, the establishment of constitutional government, the expansion of new education over the whole country, the development of the new Buddhist sects—all these things show that the Japanese do not imitate in vain. Every current in New Japan may be inspired by the main and greater current of the West, yet in a fundamental sense it is also the outcome of an inner necessity in the Japanese themselves. The same is true of their philosophy. The practical tendency of the Japanese does not hinder them in their philosophical development, though it may lay them open to the danger of clinging too closely to concrete things and of thus weakening the wings of reflection for flight above the ordinary world. Otherwise there is no reason for distrusting the ability and the true interest of the Japanese in the study of philosophy.

To conclude, the Japanese are remarkably young. In the first place, they are young in the sense of being immature. In the field of philosophy they are still in the stage of assimilation, though they have reached the stage of production in the field of science. In the second place, they are young in the sense that they are eager and untiring for new things which are good and useful. They look forward rather than backward, and they ardently desire to free themselves from the tyranny of the present. Whence comes this childlike and forward-looking attitude of the Japanese? It may come partly from the unconscious, vital energies of their youthful mind. But it originates chiefly in their self-conscious activities. The Japanese are aware of their own immaturity and shortcomings. They have a keen sense of dissatisfaction with their present state, and ardently desire to go forth towards a new region of higher ideals. For this reason we may safely say that the Japanese have a promising future. And so long as their heart is simple and their mind is unprejudiced, like a child, so long as they are thus ardent to build up that strength of mind which apprehends and cleaves to great universal truths, and so long as they are striving for an elevation of mind that may make possible higher or truer ideals, they need not, we may believe, trouble themselves with the question that has been raised by some foreign critics as to whether they possess the added gift of originality. If we humble ourselves by self-knowledge and love human souls with genuine interest as Socrates did; if we consecrate our mental endeavors in imitation of Spinoza; and if we strive diligently and regularly without haste and without rest through our whole life as did Immanuel Kant; then, what does it matter whether we have originality or not? Originality, in fine, is rather a fruit of development, than a necessary and essential factor. If we develop our minds we shall be able to produce something which is original. What we Japanese or other nations need, therefore, is self-knowledge and the struggle for the realization of higher ideals, adopting all good means for this end. We need not, nay, even ought not, to waste life in doubts and fears of any kind. We need only to be true and earnest—spending ourselves on the work before us with sincere and consecrating attitude, well assured that the right performance of this hour's duties will be the best preparation for the hours or ages that follow it. "Man's highest virtue," Goethe has said, "is always, so far as may be possible, to rule external circumstances, and as little as possible to be ruled by them." Although we cannot ignore the power of heredity, chance and environment, yet we may be convinced that it is our self-conscious activity which is the determining factor of our future destiny.

BIBLIOGRAPHY

*Okuma, S.: Fifty Years of Japan. (1909)
*Knox, G. W.: A Japanese Philosopher. (1892)
*Knox, G. W.: Japanese Life in Town and Country. (1908)
*Knox, G. W.: The Spirit of the Orient. (1906)
Mujakawa, M.: Life of Japan. (1907)
*Gulick, S. L.: Evolution of the Japanese. (4th ed. 1905)
*Nitobe, I.: Bushido. (12 ed. 1907) [Translated from English into Japanese, German, French and other languages.]
*Nitobe, I: Japanese Nation. (1912)
Uchimura, K.: Representative Men of Japan. (1908)
Uchimura, K.: How I Became a Christian.
Clement, E. W.: A Hand Book of Modern Japan. (6th ed. 1905)
*Americana (Encyclopaedia). [Articles concerning Japan are written by Professor Ladd and other scholars.]
Hearn, L.: Kokoro.
Dyer, H.: Dai Nippon. (1904)
Slead, A.: Japan by the Japanese.
Slead, A.: Great Japan. (1905)
Griffis, W.: Mikado's Empire. (11th ed. 1906)
Griffis, W.: Japanese Nation in Evolution. (1907)
Scherer: Japan To-Day. (1904)
Scherer: Young Japan. (1905)
Suimatsu: The Rising Sun. (1905)
Lloyd: Everyday Japan. (1906)
Tyndal: Japan and Japanese. (1910)
Watson: Future of Japan. (1907)
Ransome, S.: Japan in Transition. (1899)
Hitomi: Le Japon (Paris, 1900)
Harada, T.: The Faith of Japan. (1914)
* Those thus marked are of especial importance.

www.ingramcontent.com/pod-product-compliance
Lightning Source LLC
Chambersburg PA
CBHW020432010526
44118CB00010B/540